Solomon Charles Frederick Peile, Richard Dudley Sears

Lawn Tennis As a Game of Skill

With Latest Revised Laws as Played by the Best Clubs

Solomon Charles Frederick Peile, Richard Dudley Sears

Lawn Tennis As a Game of Skill
With Latest Revised Laws as Played by the Best Clubs

ISBN/EAN: 9783744736725

Printed in Europe, USA, Canada, Australia, Japan

Cover: Foto ©Lupo / pixelio.de

More available books at **www.hansebooks.com**

LAWN TENNIS

AS A GAME OF SKILL

*WITH LATEST REVISED LAWS AS PLAYED
BY THE BEST CLUBS*

BY

LIEUT. S. C. F. PEILE

B.S.C.

EDITED BY

RICHARD D. SEARS

NEW YORK
CHARLES SCRIBNER'S SONS
1885

PREFACE TO THE AMERICAN EDITION.

MR. PEILE, in treating lawn tennis as a game of skill, seems to me to have written what should be of substantial service to those who care to devote some time and pains to a thorough understanding of the game, and to the improvement of their play ; and I am glad to accept the invitation of the publishers to add a few notes suggested by my own experience, and to commend Mr. Peile's book to American tennis players.

It is hardly necessary to speak of the rapid progress the game has made in this country. Every one even in a remote degree interested in out-of-door sports has marked its growing popularity, until now every section has its tennis clubs, its "crack" players who first vie with each other for local championships, and later on put in an appearance at the national tournaments which occur each summer at Newport, to try their skill with the best players in the country.

It has often been said, and very truly, that games cannot be learnt from books, or, at all events, that the knowledge gained from books profiteth a man nothing if not supplemented by actual experience. This book is written simply to help the player to an understanding of the science of the game, to point out faults to which even expert players are sometimes addicted, and to lead the reader to direct and develop what skill he may be possessed of.

Although Mr. Peile writes for English players, who have established the game wherever England has possessions, his good advice applies with equal force to all players everywhere, the laws which govern the game being always the same. The few slight differences between the rules adopted by the English and American associations were revised only a short time ago to agree with each other.

R. D. SEARS.

Boston, July 20, 1885.

CONTENTS.

LAWN TENNIS.

I.—HINTS TO BEGINNERS.

IN compiling a few hints and suggestions for the benefit of the inexperienced player, I cannot do better than begin with the "service." The first rule in serving—and one that is much disregarded—is that "one foot must be on the baseline and the other foot behind that line, but not necessarily upon the ground."

There are, generally speaking, three sorts of "service," which admit, of course, of variations:

1. The over-hand service.
2. The under-hand service, with twist or cut.
3. The "plain" service, delivered with the arm in as nearly a horizontal position as possible.

I should myself incline to think that the over-hand service, if delivered hard and effectively, is the best, as it is difficult to "place" in the return ; but I should recommend beginners to give each sort of service a fair trial, and then adopt the one which they can, with the greatest certainty, get over the net with sufficient pace, screw, or cut on to prevent the adversary from doing "what he likes with it."

You see many players attempt a terrifically hard service the first time, which seldom escapes being a "fault" ; they then toss their second service over in such a manner that it is almost a certain "ace" for their opponents. . The inutility of a very easy service is more noticeable in a single than in a double game, as in the former there is, of course, greater opportunity for "placing."

This erratic first service, followed by an easy second one, is a great, though very common, mistake. It would be much better to give a moderately difficult service the first time ; and this, with practice, can be acquired by almost any player.

To players of some experience, I would venture to offer the following advice : Try to cultivate a useful second service, in case of the first one being a fault.

As I am, however, writing more for the benefit of beginners, I will try to explain—though it is not easy to do so without diagrams—the position the body and limbs should assume while delivering the three different sorts of service alluded to :

1. *The Over-hand Service.*

Throw the ball up to the point that the centre of your bat reaches, when held above your head. Throw it rather to the right front, and then cut at it from left to right. This " cut," though rather diminishing the pace of the ball, will help it to remain in court, and, if properly executed, will cause it to swerve slightly before bounding, and afterwards to twist to your own left, or, of course, to the adversary's right. This I look upon as the service most to be depended on, if you do

not try to force too much pace on it ; if a " fault,"
repeat the same process, rather more slowly.
This was the service affected by the Messrs. Renshaw last year at Wimbledon, where I was fortu-
nate enough to see them play.

2.   *The Under-hand Twist Service.*

Let the ball drop low, to within, say 10 inches
of the ground, rather to your right front ; bend
the body, and cut at it from right to left : this
will cause the ball to twist to your right, or to the
adversary's left, after the bound.   The back-hand
service should be delivered in much the same
manner, except that the ball need not be dropped
quite so low, and, of course, the cut administered
will be from left to right, causing the ball to twist,
after the bound, towards the adversary's right.   I
have noticed that lady-players are, as a rule, much
puzzled by a " twister" ; they would do well to
remember that a ball struck by the adversary
front - handed (in contradistinction to back-

handed) must twist to their own left, while a ball struck back-handed will invariably twist to their right. After a little training the eye will get accustomed to the amount of twist put on, and allowance and change of position should be made accordingly.

3. *The Plain Service with a Straight Arm.*

To those who cannot master either of the preceding services, I would recommend the plain service, with the arm in a horizontal position. Throw the ball about a foot away from you, rather to the front, and strike for just above the top of the net. If you see your adversary has taken up his position on the right side of the court, try to place your service to the left ; and, conversely, if he is on the left, put the ball to the right : if he is in the centre, always try to give him one which he will require to take back-hand. No great pace can be put on to this service ; so you must try to make it as difficult as possible by placing it.

A short sharp cut downwards on the ball will have the effect of making it shoot—this is the " cut" in contradistinction to the " twist."*

There are many variations of service, of course : the over-hand hard thump down without cut, though this seldom results in aught but a fault ; the slow over-hand twist ; the slow under-hand twist ; and the ordinary toss service, which is most disastrous with a good adversary, but is much in vogue with ordinary players after they have served a fault.

To take the Service.—You will see many beginners place themselves on the extreme left of the court in order, as they say, to avoid getting the ball to their back-hand. This is most unwise, as, if the server gives a sharp one to the right corner of the court, they cannot arrive in time to take it. Similarly, others go to the extreme right

---

* However, as a general rule, it is better in the long run to play the ball simply without twist or cut, but paying the greatest attention to hitting it low over the net and placing it advantageously.—AM. ED.

of the court, when they will probably get a sharp one to their back-hand.

The best position for ordinary service is a yard or so behind the service-line towards the centre of the court. If the service is very swift, it will be found necessary to stand close up to the "base-line," and sometimes even beyond it.

If your adversary serves No. 1 service with a break to the right, you may stand a foot more to the right. If he serves front-hand twisters, stand a foot to the left of the centre of the court, and rather nearer in, as twist service generally falls short. If back-hand twisters, stand a foot to the right of the centre, still near in. If he serve plainly with a straight arm, stand to a foot or two, according to the pace he puts on, behind the centre of the service-line of your court.*

---

* It is much better to stand too far back than too near, as it is easier to play a ball running forward than backward. In returning a ball, the beginner would do well to bear in mind that he should lean forward, putting the weight of his body into the stroke. If he

Ask your partner to look out for faults, as you require all your attention to take the ball. If it is doubtful whether a ball is a fault or not, do not stop to consider, but take it, as thereby disputes are saved. If a fault, you do no harm by taking it ; if not a fault, the play continues.

II.—COMMON FAULTS.

After instructing the beginner in the process of serving, there are certain common faults (in the extended sense of the word) which it is necessary to warn him against. He will do well to bear in mind perpetually the following points : Never apologize by saying you "thought the ball was not going to come over the net ;" it is your

---

leans back, he is apt to send the ball up in the air instead of low. In playing a back-handed stroke, he should learn to cross his *right* leg in front of his left, so that the side of his body is toward the net, thus giving him a greater reach and more control over the stroke. After practice he will find this back-handed stroke as easy as the fore-handed.—AM. ED.

duty not to think, but to place yourself in such a position that, if the ball does come over, you can take it. Be on your watch against the mistake of not "starting in time." A ball will come over the net and bound, and then, and not till then, do some players make a frantic rush, wildly, all arms and legs, dive at the ball, and either send it flying out of court, bang it into the net, or give such an easy return that a cool and collected adversary will demolish it. No sprawling player of this description can ever "place" a ball, or, except by a fluke, give a difficult return. A sprawler is generally a person whose occupations, before he took to this noble exercise, were sedentary. He has never played rackets or cricket, or he would know by intuition where the ball was going the moment it was struck. Now, ladies, do not accuse me of calling you "sprawlers," for, as you will see, I have purposely applied the masculine "he" to that class of player ; moreover, of course, you could not sprawl. But as I have noticed that, with a few exceptions, ladies never seem to know where the ball is going, and as they hardly ever attempt to take up their position for the return-stroke until it has either bounded or is well on its way over the net, and that then and only then they make a "start," and as often as not fail in their attempt to reach that "horrid ball," I attach a few simple hints for their benefit, and hope they may be of use to them as well as to the "sprawlers :"

Watch your adversary well : the position of his bat with respect to his body, and the direction of his eye.

If the bat is behind his body as he strikes the ball front - handed, he can only send it either straight to his front or to his right. If the bat is in front of his body as he strikes (front-handed), he will send the ball to his own left.

Similarly back-handed : if he strikes the ball while it is on a level with, or behind, his body, he must send it either straight or to his own left. If it is in front of him, he will send it to his right.

There are players who can disguise by their

motions where they are going to send the ball ; but by watching their eye you will generally be able to tell where the ball will go, as they will almost invariably look last at that spot to which they intend to send it. There are very few players who can look one way and send the ball another. This might lead to the question whether a glass eye might not be an advantage, but I think, on the whole, not.

Another essential for " starting in time" is to keep cool and collected ; make no violent rushes, but balance yourself on the ball of either foot in such a manner that you can start as readily to the right as to the left, or *vice versâ*.

How effectually a player is stumped by being caught on the " wrong foot" ! This naturally leads us on to the following " ruse" : Say you have driven a player into the corner of his left court, and he is starting quickly back again to regain his original position, thinking you will naturally send it to his right court, as that is vacant ; watch him well, and as you see him start to his right, send the ball sharp back to the left court, and you will almost for a certainty make an ace; as, if he has really started, he will be "on the wrong foot," and unable to recover himself in time to get the ball. This is a very common trick, so look out for its being practised against yourself. If you find yourself in this awkward position, make a start for the right court, but do it warily, and in such a manner that you can recover yourself at once, and get to the left, if, contrary to your expectations, the ball is returned there ; or, better still, "*pretend*" to make a violent rush to your right, and thus "induce" your adversary to send it to the left, when, being prepared for this, you will have no difficulty in returning the ball ; or, if your backhand is weak, pretend to "lag" in the left court, and this will most probably induce him to send you one in the right court, for which you will, of course, have started as soon as he has struck the ball. By feints like this you can often induce your adversary to send the ball to the very place you wish him to, and thus, without his knowing it, gain a decided advantage over him in the rally, as you can now begin to "see-saw" him, instead of his see-sawing you. By the term "see-saw" I mean driving a player first to one, and then to the other side of his court, until you tire him out, or score the ace.

Another very common fault is that of trying to "kill" a difficult ball, or trying to send back a difficult or hard-cut return every time. This is more often than not committed by racket-players who are beginning lawn tennis. They *will* look upon the game as too easy, and forget that they have not a back wall to help them. I am not saying, mind, that lawn tennis is a more difficult game than rackets, for, of course, the palm must rest with the latter in every way ; but still the absence of a back and side walls is an important factor that some people persist in forgetting ; and this renders it impossible at times to send back a severe return. When you are "tucked up" or "in a hole," the best and safest return is one tossed high in the air, and into the back of the opponent's court, thus giving yourself time not only to recover, but to see what your adversaries are going to do. Many players scorn this play, and call it an old woman's game, but it is often the only way to win. They, on the contrary, when they get a difficult ball, try to send it back hard and low with a cut on it, and the consequence is they either bang it into the net, or send it flying out of court.

What a number of games are lost by want of patience and this non-recognition of the difficulty of the game, or, in other words, want of knowledge of "how to play lawn tennis"!

Have you never, my reader, played against a man you thought you could easily beat, and found to your horror that, though an elderly man perhaps, and with nothing like your own execution, yet somehow or other he managed to beat you, chiefly—when you come to think over it afterwards—by "patience" and "placing"? You cut back at him the most difficult strokes; he returned the ball high in the air, and then at last you lost patience, and cut one into the net.

There is a class of player who often beats a better player, simply by patience; but he could never win were only the better player to be equally patient and not try to do too much, but, awaiting his chance till he got an easy one, bang it down.   This is the very essence of the game— "waiting till you get a good chance."   If you "place" carefully and with judgment, hit fairly hard, but not *too* hard, you are sooner or later sure to get your "chance," and then, with all your might, "a Renshaw smash," and good-by to the inferior player, however patient he may be.

III. — COURTS, NETS, AND APPURTE-NANCES.

In England I have only seen two sorts of "court": the "lawn," on which all matches are played—and disused "rinks," either covered or open, which come in very handy in winter, or when the grass is too wet. There are several of these old rinks in and about London, and a good deal of play goes on at them. I would recommend any one in town, who is really fond of lawn tennis, to join the "All England" Club, which owns the ground at Wimbledon ;* he is sure by that means to get a good ground to play on and good players to play with. The "Richmond" is a good club, and a good deal of lawn tennis is played there too ; the "Marylebone" is,

---

* It is to be regretted that we have in America no organization which corresponds to this "All England" Club. However, anyone who desires to watch scientific play may be reasonably sure of finding fine games in progress at the grounds of the Longwood Club, Boston ; the Young America Club, Philadelphia ; the St. George Cricket Club, Hoboken, New Jersey ; the Staten Island Cricket and Base Ball Club, New Brighton, Staten Island, N.Y., or at the Casino, Newport, during the season. All of these grounds are fitted with turf courts. Of late, and particularly in this country, "dirt" or clay courts have become popular. The "Far and Near" Club, for example, have all their courts at Hastings on the Hudson made of clay, but the hard and perfectly kept turf court must still be deemed the best adapted for scientific lawn tennis.—AM. ED.

of course, more of a cricket club, and, besides, takes a long time to get into. There are, however, any number of clubs ; in fact their name is legion, as can be seen by taking up any paper and looking at the lawn tennis engagements. In India, however, where it is, in many places, difficult to grow good grass, there are various kinds of courts. I suppose Agra and Calcutta for the Bengal Presidency can boast the best "lawns." Allahabad has a goodly number of private *pucka* courts, some of them of Portland cement, and very fast true courts they make, though, of course, the quickness of the play renders it quite a different game to the grass one, and they are also more tiring to the feet. In Lucknow the courts are chiefly of *chunam,* or of beaten earth and cowdung. The *chunam* courts are not so fast as the Portland cement ones, but more lively, if I may use that expression, the ball bounding as high as your head, for no apparent reason. The "mud" courts play more like grass ; but as the upper layer gets powdery through exposure to the sun, a ball, with a good deal of cut on, will very often not bounce at all, but shoot along the ground in a most impossible manner. In hill stations various devices are resorted to for the manufacture of courts, fine gravel being the chief element in their composition. Nothing, in my opinion, can come up to a good velvety lawn (a rare thing in India, you will say!), which is soft to the feet and kindly to the eye, with the possible exception of a "coir-matting" court. Long strips of coir-matting stitched together, and well stretched, make a perfect court, combining all the element of speed and trueness, which is so extolled by those who have Portland cement courts, with all the pleasantness of play on, enjoyed by the owner of a good grass court.

It would be invidious to say that one maker of bats and balls is better than another; all makers can turn out good bats, and the best plan is to go and overhaul their stock until you find a bat that you "feel" you can play with. Personally, I think a plain strung bat, nearly straight, but yet with a slight curve, a roughened wooden handle, and heavy rather than light, is the best style of bat ; but of course, on this, as on most subjects, opinions differ.* . . .

Courts.—Reverting to courts, I think at least 15 ft. should be allowed behind either base-line, and 10 ft. at the sides, where it is possible to do so.† Some people have a tree, say 7 ft. behind one of the back courts ; others a bush ; while in another court the level alters at that distance, and there is a " drop" ; this last is the most dis-

---

* Many of the best English and American experts will not agree in the author's preference for a heavy racket. Much the larger number among the best players, including both champions of England and America, prefer medium weight bats, ranging from 14 to 15 oz. Readers will find that a racket with an octagon handle, which is now sometimes made in this country, is much firmer in the hand than the old style handle after the player once becomes accustomed to the rather sharp edges of the wood. However, use always the racket that suits your personal requirements best.—AM. ED.

† This is a point upon which too much stress cannot be laid. The player who is obliged to protect a court which has less than 15 ft. level sward back of the baseline is seriously handicapped at the outset.—AM. ED.

tressing of all, for not only is it a severe shock to
the system to drop down a foot or two unawares,
but it spoils one's play to have to be perpetually
on the look-out for pitfalls.   I think that 15 ft.
at either end, and 10 at the sides, is the minimum
that should be allowed.   Of course in some
places, where there is a great scarcity of level
ground, one must make the best of a bad job,
and avoid tumbling down if possible. The "net"
should be 3 ft. in the centre, and 3 ft. 6 in. at
the sides.   How often one sees nets that are "all
height"—perhaps 2 ft. 6 in. at the centre, and
4 ft. at the sides ; and how utterly destructive of
good play this is !   Cavendish's patent "net arrangement," with wheel and ratchet, is of course
the best.* The simplest and most effective system
next to it that I have seen is the following : Get
two stout poles, about 7 ft. in length and 6 in. in

* The Cavendish " net arrangement" may be obtained from any dealer in lawn tennis goods. Another
very excellent device has been invented and patented
by Dr. J. Dwight.—AM. ED.

diameter; fix them firmly in the ground, so that
3 ft. are buried, leaving 4 ft. standing out.   At
3 ft. 6 in. from the ground bore a hole about 1
in. in diameter; in this hole a carpenter can
easily fix a small wheel.   Pass the rope on which
the net is now suspended through either hole,
and haul it up till the net is about 3 ft. 3 in.
high at the centre; fasten the ends of the rope
to a stake in the ground on the outside of either
post.   Now get an iron fork made in
this shape, the upright portion being
exactly 3 ft. high; put this fork over
the net at point a, and drive the forked
portion down until b and c are flush
with the ground.   Your net will now
be 3 ft. in the centre, and 3 ft. 6 in. at
either side, and nothing short of an
earthquake will alter it.

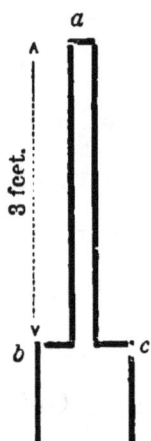

Ayres' white balls are the best, and preferable
by far to the red, or parti-colored red and white
balls one sees used at some courts.   There is a
ball now made and much used, called, I think,

"the enamelled ball": this is an uncovered glazed ball, of the same size and weight as the match-ball, and is exceedingly convenient for rainy weather, as you simply have to rub the ball with a wet cloth, and it comes out as good as new. Of course they are a little more lively than the covered ones, but are decidedly preferable to old, dirty, or sodden-covered balls.

IV.—GENERAL PRINCIPLES AND CLUB RULES.

There are many indifferent players who say, " I don't play well ; I have got to a certain point, and shall never get any better." Now these should remember that practice makes perfect. They have copied that phrase out many times as children ; why cannot they apply it now ? If a player *really* practises he *must* improve. It can hardly be called " practice" to go on perpetually making the same mistakes, and finally getting

thoroughly disgusted with one's self. What are
required are patience, good temper, and a critical
examination of one's own play and faults. Fail-
ing these, no player can expect to improve his
game. He has got to a " certain point "—by dint
of playing, I suppose—for it is to be presumed he
now plays better than he did when he first began.
Why cannot he then get a point further ? I am
afraid he does not really try ; he gives it up as a
hopeless job. He always serves his first attempt
a fault ; let him try a less difficult service, until
he gets sufficiently good, by practising this easier
one, to increase the pace, put on more " cut," or
to be able to try the more difficult service with a
reasonable chance of success. By-and-by he will
be able to get it over the first time for nearly a
certainty, and then he can practise for a yet more
difficult service, and so on. There are certain
strokes he always fails in ; he gives up hope, or
gets impatient, and consequently always fails at
this particular stroke. Let him try to " return"
it with less pace on at first, until he succeeds in

getting it over ; then he can put it back a little harder, and so on, gradually improving his play in the points in which he is weak. The first essential is concession of weakness ; the second is capability of observing where the weakness lies ; the third, patience to overcome that weakness ; and the last, practice to annihilate it. Any player working on this system is bound to improve, unless, of course, he has some physical unfitness for the game ; and then, of course, he can only strive to minimise as much as possible the effect of that infirmity. There are some players, of course, who are naturally more fitted for the game than others, but there is no reason why the latter should lose heart ; they will not make the rapid strides at first that the former do ; but still they will go on improving, until some day, perhaps, through carelesness or laziness on the part of the former, they may put the moral of the fable concerning "the hare and the tortoise" into practical effect. *Nil desperandum* should be the motto of lawn tennis : the indifferent players should strive to get better ; the good ones should remember that the game is at present in its infancy, and that they may, like Mr. Renshaw, evolve out of their inner consciousness some style of play that will annihilate even the "All England Champion." Personally, I believe that with a lawn tennis as with a billiard ball, "anything can be done ;" and were professionals to take to the game, we should see feats performed that are not even dreamt of now. So let every player live in hope—the beginner emulating the veteran, and the fine player trying to put on some screw or cut that will render the ball untakable.

There seems to be an idea prevalent in some places (I am speaking here chiefly of India) that lawn tennis on public courts should be legislated for as rackets is—*i.e.*, that players should "cut in" strictly according to seniority of arrival on the ground. This is a very good rule theoretically, but is, in practice, conducive to the formation of bad and unequal games. It seems to me, too, that rackets and lawn tennis are hardly analogous.

There are only one, or perhaps two, racket courts for all the players, and naturally rules must be strict, or the "duffers" would not have a chance. In lawn tennis it is different. There are at most public grounds a large number of courts, quite sufficient to admit of more than half the people present playing at the same time; and I do not see why some arrangement should not be come to which would make the games as even as possible; and in this way surely more enjoyment could be got out of the game than can be under the rule of the slate? Why make hard-and-fast rules, like the laws of the Medes and Persians? Let there be rules for general guidance; but if players wish to accommodate one another by exchanging, and thereby making two even, instead of two uneven games, let them be allowed to do so. For instance, in No. 1 court there are four players, one of whom is good, the others indifferent; in No. 2 court there are three good, and one indifferent player. Why make such rules as to *condemn* eight men to play an uninteresting, because unequal game, the whole afternoon ? Let the good player in No. 1 court exchange with the indifferent one in No. 2 court, and two good and even-sided games will be obtained. Let a player, if he so choose, sit out a game, if thereby a better game can be obtained next time, and do not penalise him for so doing, as I have seen done at some courts, by making the wretched man go to the very bottom of the list.

If exchanges of this sort once became general enough to be the custom, and if they were carried out in a proper spirit and in accordance with the general sense of the players, really good games would always be obtainable on public grounds. It must be remembered that one good player spoils a game for three poor ones just as much, if not more, than a bad player spoils a game for three good ones. Of course, exchanging and sitting out can be carried too far and the system abused ; but public opinion and the honorary secretary ought to be strong enough to re-

press any tendency of this sort on the part of tur-
bulent spirits. In many stations in India the
custom I have proposed exists, and the system is
found to work satisfactorily—everybody doing his
utmost to promote the interests of the game
and the happiness of players by helping to form
as equal-sided sets as possible.

V.—THE SINGLE GAME.

Great argument is, I believe, now going on
as to the respective merits of the different styles
of play — the volley and the back game. I
cannot see how there can be any argument in
the matter at all, and think, and am going to
try to prove, that a man who volleys from a
position at a distance of 1 ft. behind the service-
line, must beat an equal player, whose normal
position is at the back of the court.* Of course

----

* Mr. Renshaw and several other well-known players take a position even in advance of that recommended

if you can play the back game very well, and
cannot volley at all, it would be ridiculous for you
to attempt the volley game in a match. Volleying is merely a question of practice.*. . . And if
you have a fair eye, you will soon find that you
are able to volley just as easily, and place balls
better than you formerly could from the bound.†
Now get a piece of paper and mark out a court
on it, draw a dotted line one foot behind the
service-line in the single court and parallel to
it, and remember that this is the line you have
to defend at a volley. We will call this dotted

---

by the author, *i.e.*, 3 ft. in front of the service-line.
If you stand too far back it gives your opponent a
chance to put the ball at your feet, thus making a hard
stroke which otherwise might be an easy return.—AM.
ED.

* Make up your mind that you will master it.—AM.
ED.

† The experience of Mr. H. L. Lawford is a strong argument in favor of the volley game. For some years
Mr. Lawford was known as the finest base line player;
but finding that Mr. W. Renshaw invariably beat him,
he has adopted the volleying tactics, declaring that it
is the play to win.—AM. ED.

line, for the sake of easy reference, the "volleying line." Draw diagonals from corner to
corner of your court, and note where they in-
tersect your volleying line. You will now see
that by playing up so much closer to the net you
will have, for five balls out of six, less than two-
thirds of the ground to cover that your adversary
has, who plays from near the back-line. Note,
too, that from your forward position you can see
much more of the game than he can. The only
balls that can make you run much are those returned from the corner of the right or left court
in a direction parallel with, and near to, either
side-line. The best way to guard against a return of this sort is to go a little to the left of the
centre of your volleying line when your adversary
has the ball in the corner of his right court, and
vice versâ a little to the right of the centre when
he has the ball in his left corner. But do not go
so much to either side as to enable him to put it
past you on the other side. Note by your diagram
that any balls hit diagonally across the court will

pass your volleying line not very far from the centre ; so the best general position to take up is about the middle of your dotted line, and always try to *regain* your place there if you have temporarily lost it during a rally. Note, too, that by your forward position you are within easy reach of any ball dropped gently over the net, while such balls would in all probability prove too much for your back-line adversary — more especially if you drive him well back in the first instance (which is very easy to do if he will not volley), and then drop a gentle one just over. You are sufficiently back, besides ; for most high balls, hit over your head so that you cannot reach them, will probably go out of court. You have this further advantage over your adversary—that while you can drive him back till he is almost behind the back-line and then drop a gentle one just over the net, he cannot well do the same to you ; for *you*, in all probability, intercept his ball at a volley that otherwise would have driven *you* back , and not having lost your position,

you are close enough to the net to deter him
from attempting the ruse of a gentle one. Of
course, he may make an unexpectedly good
stroke that will drive you back, and having done
so, if he is a good player, he will try to keep you
there ; but even then you are on equal terms with
him, until you can regain your position on the
volleying line, when you will again have the advantage over him. Playing against a man who
also volleys, your great object is, by placing, to
either get the ball past him or to drive him back,
and to keep him back. Sooner or later, unless
your adversary is a very fine player, you will get
an easy chance, as, from your position, you can
easily run in and smash a loose ball ; but until
you get a *good* chance, play cautiously, and with
your head ; place the balls as much as possible
from right to left, or to some undefended spot,
so as to keep your adversary, even though a
volleyer, on the run, and the odds are, you get
your chance soon enough ; but when it comes,
be careful you do not miss it, but place the ball

carefully, and hard, to some part of the court that your adversary cannot get to, in preference to "smashing" at it wildly, whereby you would probably only put the ball into the net, and thus lose a golden opportunity. Another point — and this is most important — is, that the moment you have delivered your service you should *follow it up*, and take position on the "volleying line" to, if possible, volley the return. Say you are serving from the right court. Deliver your service, and at once run to about a foot to the left of the centre of your volleying line. Your adversary returns the ball : now, if you can volley it sharp, hard, and well back into his left court, it will be an almost certain ace for you, as, having had to take your service in his right court, he will hardly be quick enough to get over to the left in time to reach the ball. Note again by volleying how quick your return is ; it is probably "past" your back-line adversary before he knows where he is ; whereas, while "he" is waiting for the ball to "bound," you have ample time not only to watch what he is going to do, but to take up any position you may consider best suited for his return. We will suppose you are now taking a service in your right court. Remember, to deliver it, your adversary is also in his right court : consequently your best return is into his left court, making the ball go parallel and as close to the side-line on your right as possible ; then run immediately and take your position about a foot to the right of the centre of your volleying line, as the ball will, of course, be returned from his *left* court. Personally, I think the argument is all one-sided ; everything is in favor of the volleyer, while I cannot see anything that rests with his opponent, except it be the statement that "it is easier to return a ball from the bound than at the volley," and this I take leave to doubt. Note again that by volleying you prevent any cut or twist the ball may have on from acting ; while, if you wait for it to bound, you get the whole force of any cut or twist there may be on it, and run the risk of getting a shooter—or, if there are any inequalities in the ground, of a false bound, or of the ball jumping as high as your head, which last, when you do not expect it, is most difficult to return. I do not say that you *must* volley every ball—that would be impossible ; but volley as much as you can. Take every possible opportunity of doing so, and I think you will soon find yourself far ahead of your back-line friends. The mistake made at first by beginners at volleying is either that they are nervous, and remain too far back to volley properly, or else that they are too confident, and come too close to the net. This latter fault is most fatal, as if you are too near the net a steady adversary will be sure to put the ball quickly past you on either side, so that you cannot reach it, or will toss it over your head to the back of the court, when you have not only to run back for it, but probably also to turn, and the chances are you send back an easy return, and not being able to regain position, or being out of breath, you lose an ace. Another great fault of beginners is, that they forget to follow up their service, thus not only losing the advantage of position on the volleying line, but also giving their adversary a wide court in which to place the ball, and an opportunity of keeping them back. The man at the net has no chance in a single game, and I am going to attempt to prove in my No. VI. that this is not a good position for a player, even in a double game.

VI.—THE DOUBLE GAME.

There are, generally speaking, three ways of playing a double game : (1) the old style, in which both players remain in the back of the court ; (2) where one player is up near the net, while his partner takes the back of the court ; (3) where the partners stand side by side on the volleying line (or one foot behind the service-line). * and

---

* See note on page 36.

volley as much as they can, as in a single game. I
will not deal much with the old style of play ; it
is getting obsolete, and this is in some ways a great
pity, as one used to see long and very exciting ral-
lies of perhaps fifty or sixty returns. Volleying
has now knocked these on the head, and they exist
no more. As we must move with the times, we will
go on to No. 2 game, in which one man plays up,
the other back. This game is the one most in
vogue in India now, and here we get the elements
of the " man at the net." I will first try to demon-
strate how this style of game should be played,
and then to prove that where both players volley
as in No. 3 style, their tactics are far superior to
those of No. 2 game. We will first suppose that
you are the forward player, and that your partner
is serving from the right court. Go close up to the
net for the first service, if he serves well, as you
will then be able to kill a loose ball ; but take
care that you do not leave sufficient room at your
outer side (*i.e.*, the side further from your partner) to allow of the adversaries placing the ball

past you there. If the first service is a fault, drop back a bit, to about the service-line, as the second will probably be an easy one, and therefore the chances are against your adversaries sending a loose return. Sometimes if you make a feint of going to the right, as if you were going to poach your partner's ball, it may induce your opponent to send the ball to the left of you, when, if you are strong at a back-hand volley, being prepared for this, you may get a chance of sending back a severe return ; or this feint, if made at the last moment, may frighten your adversary, if he is nervous, into sending the ball so much to your right or left as to make it go out of court. Sometimes, *when you get a good chance,* make a real rush to the right, and poach from your partner, but do not do this often. Doing so every now and then will make your feints of more effect than if you never poached at all. When you run across like this, your partner, as I will show further on, should go to his left, and cover the blank space left by you in the court. Thus sometimes poaching, sometimes making a feint, you will put the other side out considerably, and unless they are cool, collected players, may score a few aces by these means. Shift your position a good deal, and never get into the habit of standing stock-still in one place. If you remain stationary, your adversaries will know where you are, and can put the ball past you ; while if you keep moving, even though slightly, it will puzzle them. Always take care, as a forward player, to guard your outer side, as your partner cannot help you there, though he can take any ball that passes you on your inner side (or that side of you on which he is). Keep to your own side as much as possible, and do not be perpetually crossing your partner and taking his balls. When you do get an easy chance, however, make up your mind, even though it be poaching, and run and smash the ball. If the adversaries get angry, and hit hard at you, notice how the ball is coming, and if it is on the rise, as it reaches you, dodge on one side, and, if they are hitting angrily, the ball will go out of court. If one of

your adversaries is also playing up, do not send
the ball to him, unless you can hit hard at him,
but work your back adversary. Above all things,
do not get excited, but play coolly and collectedly.
When your partner is serving from the left court,
you can make feints of poaching with great advantage, as you will thus, in all probability, get
the ball sent to your right hand.

Now we will suppose that you are the back
player, and that it is your partner who is playing
up, one of the adversaries also being up. When
your partner poaches, do not stand still and abuse
him for so doing, but run across and guard the
space he has left empty. If you can only remember to do this, you will save many a rally. His
poaching is annoying, no doubt, especially if he
sends an easy return ; but never mind : do *your*
duty at any rate, and run into the unguarded
court. When you are serving, remember that it
is of infinite value to your up partner if you can
get your first service over hard, as the adversaries
will probably give him an easy return off it, which

he can smash : so try and make as few faults as possible the first time. After serving run in a foot or two, as there is a large empty space in front of you which your partner cannot guard without poaching. By coming in in this way you will be able to get gentle balls dropped just over the net, and these you would not be able to reach were you to remain standing on the spot from which you serve. Note this point, as it is a most important one. Nine players out of ten stand stock-still after serving. When your adversary does this, drop a gentle one into the front of his court. Remember, too, when you are back, not to hit at the man at the net. If he is anything like a decent player you will seldom gain, and nearly always lose an ace by so doing. Many people have told me that the man at the net has a sort of fascination for them ; that he puts them off, makes them nervous, and they cannot *help* hitting at him ; that this is more especially the case when they are taking a serve, and then of course this man is directly opposite them. I can only advise such players not to look at him ; gaze at the server, and return the ball to him. There is plenty of room. Say you are taking the service in the right court : your up adversary is immediately in front of you ; therefore you have three-quarters, or at any rate two-thirds, of the whole net on your left of him over which to hit the ball, and a wide court to place it in ; or you can toss the ball over the head of the man at the net into the court far behind him. If, however, you are not put out by this man's presence so near the net, watch him well ; and if you get a chance, put the ball on his outer side. If you can get the ball past him there, you will probably score an ace, as his partner, being in the other court, cannot help him. If he is one of that sort who, not looking after his own court, plays and keeps near the centre of the net, you will have a gay time of it, for you can place the ball on either side of him at will, or toss it over his head, and his unfortunate partner will be running to and fro, never knowing which side to go to ; and, moreover, will be much disturbed by the presence of his partner, who is right in front of him, probably just where he wants to hit the ball to. Remember this, and if you are an up player, never keep near the centre of the net, but mind your own court, and to do that properly you will have quite enough to do. If you do by any chance run to the centre to take an easy ball, get back at once to your own court after playing it; or if you know your partner, go on to the other side, and he will cover the space you have left empty. Help your partner by looking out for faults when he is taking service, and get him to do the same for you. Shout out when you are certain a ball is going out, and do so in time to prevent him from striking at the ball, not while he is in the act of striking, or else you will balk him. If you are going to poach, say "mine," or intimate that you are going to take the ball, so that he may cover the empty court in time. In fact, help your partner as much as you can in every way.

Now we will look at the game as played by two

men, who stand about a foot behind * the service-line, each in his own court, and volley. Here each player guards his own court, and there is no necessity for poaching. Each player plays as in a single game, and has, moreover, only little more than half that space to cover. Most of the balls being returned at the volley by these players, it becomes very difficult work for their adversaries, who may not be accustomed to such quick play. Here each player, after moving to take a ball, should return to his normal position. Neither player is put out by having his partner dodging about in front of him. They are both so placed that they are within easy reach of any balls dropped over the net, and they can run in and smash loose returns, while any ball put hard over their heads, so that they cannot reach it, will go out of court. They should be careful to guard each their outer side, and the man in the right court should remember that his partner's front-hand is

---

* See note on page 36.

probably stronger than his own back-hand, and
in the case of a doubtful ball should give way accordingly. If they can volley, which is, of course,
a *sine qua non* here, they can easily guard their
respective courts, and it requires a very well-hit
ball indeed to get past them. There is no empty
space left in the court, if only each player will
remember to get back to his proper position after
taking a ball. It now simply becomes a question
of how well they can play; and as they are so
placed that they can reach everything, they have
only got to return the balls, and they *must* win.
There is no confusion, no poaching, no getting
in one another's way, no getting one in front of
the other at one side of the court, and so leaving
the whole of the other side unguarded. They
leave this sort of thing to their up and back adversaries. Over two back adversaries they have
nearly, but not quite, the same advantage as a
volleyer has in a single court over a back-player.
The element of the man at the net is done away
with, as this person would have too hot a time of

it with two good volleyers so close to him. I, for one, would like to see him abolished, and I hope we shall all be able to congratulate one another before very long in having said good-by to the " man at the net."

Of course, when all four are volleyers, the two best will drive the others back, and, forcing them to play the back game, will gain the advantage.*

VII.—RULES THAT ARE OFTEN DISREGARDED. THEIR OBJECT, AND REASONS THEREOF.

Since writing the first edition of this pamphlet I have had several references made to me regard-

---

* Never change your mind at the last moment, as it proves fatal in nine cases out of ten. If you have stepped forward intending to volley the ball, and it falls so far short that it might be taken on the bound, still preserve your original intention and volley it, even if by so doing you are convinced that your first judgment was wrong. It may be accepted as an invariable rule : *Never change your mind.*—AM. ED.

ing rules, and this has induced me to add this chapter, with the object of pointing out those rules which appear to me to be generally broken, and at the same time to give a short explanation of why it is necessary they should remain in force.

Rule 2.—Here note that while the size and weight of the balls are laid down, there is no restriction as to the proportions of a bat.

Rule 7.—" The server shall serve with one foot on the base-line, with the other foot behind that line, but not necessarily on the ground," etc. This rule is perpetually disregarded, and you may often see players serving with both feet within, or perhaps with both feet beyond, the base-line. The object of the above rule is manifestly to prevent a person from serving from a position too near the net, whence he would be able to smash down the ball in a manner impossible to take.

Rule 13.—" The service may not be volleyed," etc. Very naturally not, as otherwise you could go right up to the net and kill every service. Here a decision by the " Field," June 18, 1881, may be noticed. It is : " Or if it touches an adversary (before it bounds) it is a good service." The fact of it touching that adversary, or his bat, is equivalent to his having taken it, and therefore an ace to you. Thus, at the score " vantage," if you were serving from the left court to the adversary on your right, and were by accident to hit the wrong adversary (*i.e.*, the one in the other court), it would still be an ace to you, and game. This appears hard on your opponents at first sight, but the man you hit should have got out of the way : moreover, it could only occur very seldom. Meanwhile, if the reverse held good, an unprincipled adversary might stop any very good service of yours with his foot, and claim a let, or the same thing might occur unintentionally.

Rule 14.—" The server shall not serve until the striker-out is ready." Mark this, you players who serve your second service rapidly after the first, without waiting to give your opponent any time.

Rule 21, *para.* 2.—" If he lose the next stroke"

(he being vantage), "the score is again called *deuce ;* hence there is no such score as " vantage-all"—see also the " Field," October 21, 1882. This method of scoring has evidently been invented by little local clubs, who have not enough of courts for their members, or for some reason or other— to save time, perhaps. Of course, if players like to agree to this scoring, or if, for any special reason, the committee of a club decide that " vantage-all" shall be scored, a player could hardly *claim* to have proper scoring of " back again to deuce." But if the committee do so decide, they should publish their decision before any match is played, and let it be generally known, to avoid disputes.*

Rule 22.—By this you can see that the " rule" is to play " advantage sets," though the note leaves it optional. I have seen eighteen games

---

* In the northern championship this year (1885) at Manchester, England, one set required 26 games to decide it, the score standing 14–12. This is the longest game at present on record.—AM. ED.

played in one set at Prince's, in the open handicap, before that set could be decided.

Rule 23.—It does not appear to be generally known that players can claim to change sides of every game, if either side of the court has a distinct advantage.

Rule 38.—"Nor shall the strikers-out change courts till the end of the set." This rule is broken constantly, in order, I suppose, to give each player practice in either court. It should be adhered to in matches.

DECISIONS BY THE "FIELD."

November 19, 1881.—Note that it is a fault if you *strike* at the ball and miss it.

December 3, 1881.—A player receiving 15 must commence serving in the right court. Rule 7 says "the server . . . shall deliver the ball from the right and left courts alternately, beginning from the right." Hence, no matter the points a player gets, he must begin from the right. I have heard people say that when they get 15 it is inconvenient

beginning from the right court, as the scoring and
the service do not then tally ; but I maintain that
it is this very fact that enables them to see whether
they are serving from the proper court, and acts
as a guide to the score — that is, if you have
started with 15 from the right court and the score
becomes 40—30, and you are still serving from
the right court, you ought to know you are in order, from the apparent wrongness of the score.
Similarly, "a player who takes (*i.e.*, claims) his
bisque, serves from same court he would have
served from if he had not taken it ;" and naturally so, as otherwise he would have to serve twice
running from the same court.   To revert to the
previous discussion : I think the rule is in every
way a judicious one, as, supposing the rule were
that "a player getting 15 points should begin
from the left court," he would be much more
likely to make the mistake of beginning from the
right court (which he is naturally accustomed to
do), and the umpire would be much less likely to
notice this mistake than he or the player himself

would be to make an error in the scoring, especially when they have the apparent wrongness of
score to act as their guide, as I have shown above.
I have heard this point argued over and over again
on either side in matches, and I think it a great
pity there is not always a book of rules on every
ground, for by this means all disputes would be
saved.

July 16, 1881.—"It is not a 'let' if a ball
drops on another in court."* [*Moral.*—Take care
not to leave balls lying about in your court.]

July 23.—"If you or your partner touch the
net while the ball is 'in play,' you lose the stroke
('ace')." By October 8, 1881, it can be seen that
this is a point dependent on whether the ball was
in play or not in play (see Rule 16) when the net
was touched ; not on whether the ball was or was
not properly returned.

June 24, 1884.—"If, when you volley the ball,
your racket is 'not' over the net, you do not lose

---

* Neither is it a stroke for your adversary. Return
it if you can.—AM. ED.

the stroke unless your racket follows over the net before the ball has left it,"—*i.e.*, if your racket, at the moment the ball *leaves* it, is over the net, you lose an ace. In ordinary games, without an umpire, it would be almost impossible to decide this point ; and in such practice-games it appears to me almost better to disregard this rule, and let the point be decided by whether or not the net were touched by the player in question.

July 1, 1882.—" It is a good return if the ball is played after it has twisted back past the net, provided the net is not touched while the ball is in play." Thus, you may place your racket over and past the net to take a ball, which has already bounded, but you must not (in a match) " volley" a ball, with your racket in such a position.

July 7, 1883.—The player who is touched by the ball in play loses the stroke—*e.g.* if you are standing clear out of court, and the ball hits you before it has bounded (*i.e.*, while it is in play), it is an ace to the other side.

The fact of your being out of court is no argu-

ment, as the " Field " graphically says " you may
be standing near the net, or in the *next parish.*"
[*Moral.*—Avoid the ball when it is going out of
court, even when you are out of court.]

VIII.—WHEN TO TAKE A BISQUE.

This is a point involving much careful consid-
eration. The first thing is not to forget to take
it. I have seen several matches lost by a player,
who was receiving points, forgetting to take his
bisque. The natural remark is, " How stupid of
him !" but it must be remembered that a bisque
may not be taken after the service has been delivered.*

Rule 25, *para.* 2.—A player might have meant
to take his bisque at a certain period of the game.
He forgets to do so at the required moment—
meanwhile his adversary has served ; it is like

---

* A bisque may be taken by the striker-out after a
fault, but not by the server.—Am. Ed.

claiming two by honors at whist, after the turn-up card is exposed—too late ! He is annoyed with himself for his stupidity ; his play is affected by his annoyance, and hence misfortune follows on misfortune, in compliance with the old proverb.

However, we will assume the bisque is not going to be forgotten, and then the question arises, when to take it ? First of all, do not be in a hurry to take it. It is always better to win a game with your bisque—*i.e.*, to take it when you are vantage, than at any other particular period, and it is always better, too, to take it late on in the set, than at the beginning. Of course, the very best point at which to take it is when the score is five games-all, and you are vantage in the eleventh game, as you win the set thereby, and have given your adversary not only a great deal of work, but have also inflicted on him a severe disappointment.

I will quote one or two instances, showing what I mean by reserving your bisque. Say you are

four games to your opponent's love, and 40 to his
30 in the fifth game, and are feeling pretty fit,
while your adversary seems tired : don't take your
bisque—reserve it : let him tire himself more : let
him, perhaps, tire himself completely out by winning the next two games. In the following game
either take it or not, as your judgment decides, if
you happen to get to advantage. Of course, if
you do not take it, and yet win this game, claim it
if you get to *vantage* in the next game, as that will
win you the set. But if in this, the eighth game
(score five games to two, you win), you get to 40—
15, do not claim your bisque "unless your adversary makes the next ace ;" for if you can win the
set without having taken your bisque, you will
have gained a decided moral advantage over your
opponent, as he will think he has been too heavily
handicapped with regard to you, and unless he
has a "heart," will give in, and you will probably
win the match easily. If he has pluck, however,
you have lost nothing, but have even succeeded
in pumping him a little more than you would

have done had you won the game sooner. To go back a bit : I said if you are 40—30 in the fifth game and four games to love, and are feeling pretty fit while your adversary looks tired, don't take your bisque. The reverse of this is applicable if the conditions are altered ; that is to say, if you are tired out by the time you reach the above score, and your adversary is not, take your bisque and win the fifth game. You are then five games to love, and can afford to lose two or three games for the sake of regaining your strength ; and when you have recovered, begin playing up again. This is called "saving yourself," and is a point to which sufficient attention is not given. It is like racing—don't run it too fine, but win by half a length, in preference to coming in a winner by several lengths. By the former plan you save your strength for the next sets, whereas if you go on playing up when you are thoroughly tired in order to win by an unnecessary amount, you will probably be useless in the succeeding sets. Another point at which you can save yourself with advantage is the following : Say you have won the first set, and that in the second set your adversary has scored four games to your one ; you have lost your breath, and are feeling a bit tired. Is it worth your while to utterly exhaust yourself by trying to pull this game, which is so far gone, out of the fire ? I should say *not*. Don't give in utterly, but at the same time don't tire yourself more by running after difficult balls ; try and work your adversary, with the least possible exertion to yourself. Let him win this set, but try and make him tire himself in the so doing, and try yourself to recover your spent breath and strength. In the next set the conditions will probably be altered—that is, he will be pumped, while you are fresh after your rest, and have a better chance of winning than if you were utterly exhausted. At the score of three games-all, especially in the fifth set, it is a most important thing to secure the fourth game ; and I would here recommend a player to take his bisque in the seventh game, if he gets to vantage ; and

if his adversary got to vantage, I do not think he
would be wrong to take his bisque and make the
game deuce ; but then, of course, he would have
to do his very utmost to try and win this game.
At three-all, being just half-way through the set,
it is most important to try by any means to get
the start in the second half. At the score of five
games-all, if your adversary gets to either " advantage," or is 40 to your 30, take your bisque, as it
is all-important to you, to prevent at any hazards
his winning this, the deciding game of the set.
By exercising your judgment in taking your
bisque, and also in saving yourself, you will win
many a game that a less thoughtful player would
lose. The great thing is just to hold your adversary as you would a pulling horse—feel his mouth,
keep him well in hand, and if he gets right away
with you, let him go a bit, only to take a stronger
and more effective pull at him as soon as you get
him in hand again. What I mean is this : if you
get a long way ahead of your adversary, at the
cost of a good deal of exertion to yourself, ease

off a little bit, till you regain strength sufficient
to put on a final spurt and win the game ; while,
if your adversary gets so far away from you in any
particular set that you feel it is hopeless, work
him as much as you can, but reserve your chief
effort for the next set, when you will again start
on even terms with him.*

IX.—A CHAPTER FOR LADIES.

Single Game, Played by Two Ladies.

Having been asked to add a chapter to my
" Lawn Tennis Notes" specially for the benefit of
ladies, I proceed to do so, but hope I may be ex-
cused if I go over a little old ground. I am now
only writing for the benefit of those ladies (and
there are many such, I know) who love lawn ten-

---

* Be careful not to "save" yourself too much, as you
may get your hand out and not be able to play up again,
as in the famous case of Grinstead vs. Browne.—
AM. ED.

nis as a "game of skill," and who do not play merely to kill time.

The first essential, if you wish to get to anything beyond mediocrity as a player, is to dress for the purpose. Luckily short dresses are now in fashion, so there is not much difficulty about that point; but if the fashion changes, I implore you to beware of long dresses, for two very good reasons :

1. The long dress will spoil your play; and

2. The play will spoil your long dress.

The next point to pay attention to is shoes. Of course you will wear shoes without heels, and equally, of course, will the soles be of India-rubber. A tight shoe being a disadvantage should be discarded, even though it may offer some attraction in the matter of appearance. A great big hat that waggles about is also trying to the wearer, as also are bangles, bracelets, and suchlike ornaments— not to mention five or six rings on one finger. These latter are more liable to cause blisters, by pinching up the skin between the hand and the bat, than anything I know of. We will now sup-

pose you have attired yourself in a suitable cos-
tume of cashmere or flannel, a nice small hat, and
a pair of easy-fitting shoes, and that you are about
to play a single game against a girl antagonist that
you would give worlds to beat. (I will treat of
the double game as played by two ladies on a side,
and then by a gentleman and a lady, afterwards.)

You win the toss, choose the best side, and your
adversary serves first from the right court. She
will probably go to the extreme corner of the right
of her court to serve (most ladies do, I notice).
Mark this, and return the ball, as nearly as you
can, into the left corner of her left court. There
is nothing difficult in this, if you make up your
mind to it. It is simply hitting the ball straight
in front of you. Let the ball come a little past
you on the bound and then hit it, and you can
hardly help sending it straight to your front. Remember, too, that a ball hops a good long distance.
Many people forget this, and rush to the place
where they think the ball will bound, and thus
give themselves a difficult stroke. A ball struck

in an ordinary way will bound about 6 ft.,
and at 3 ft. will be at about its highest point. It
is easier to strike a ball on the descent of its bound
than it is on the ascent ; so if you remain, or go
to, about 4½ ft. behind where you think an ordi-
narily hit ball will bound from, you will be in about
the best position to place your return. But this
is merely parenthetical, so *revenons à nos moutons.*
You have succeeded in driving the ball into the left
of your adversary's court, and have thus given her
a run from the right to the left corner. She will
probably, after her long run, give a fairly easy return, which you will be able to place into the right
corner of her right court, thus making her run
again ; or if her back-hand is weak, keep on attack-
ing it. By these tactics you will weary your adversary, and will most likely win the games in which
she serves. Of course, when she serves from the
extreme corner of her left court, you would return
the ball into her right court, and so on.

Now to come to the games in which you are
server. You have seen by the above that you

gain a distinct advantage over an adversary who chooses either extreme corner to serve from, so do not commit this mistake yourself. Serve from about 2 ft. to the right or left of the centre line of your court, as then, if your adversary returns the ball to either corner, you have only half the distance to run that you would have were you in the far corner. This is not the only advantage. By serving from near the centre of the court it is much easier for you to serve to either the front or back-hand of your adversary, as you please, than it is to do so from the corner, whence you have a natural tendency to send the ball in a similarly diagonal direction across her court each time. You will see what I mean by trying, on a court, to serve to your adversary's back-hand from the extreme corner of your right court. Try this also from near the centre, and I think you will agree with me that it is easier to do so from the latter place. Remember another point, and that is, that the greater judgment and knowledge you show in discovering where the ball will pitch, after it has been hit, the less you will have to run about. This knowledge of " where the ball will go " is less common amongst ladies than men, chiefly on account of the latter having more experience in other games, such as cricket and rackets, where it becomes a second nature to a man to know where his adversary will hit, almost before he has hit, though he could perhaps hardly explain how he arrives at this knowledge. It is a sort of subtle instinct born of judgment and observation, and matured by practice. It can only be acquired by patiently watching how each ball is struck, and noticing, by the effort made by the striker, the amount of force put on the ball ; and by watching from the lie of his bat with respect to his body, and the inclination of his sight (as detailed in Chapter II.), the direction in which the ball will be sent. Again, I must hark back to where you have delivered your service from nearly the centre of the court. If you have acquired the knowledge just described you will guess where your adversary will send the ball, and will be there in time to re-

turn it with effect, and perhaps to establish your
attack, in the same manner as you did when she
was serving. But if you have not acquired this instinct, you must do the best you can, and with ac-
tivity, backed up by an ability to place the ball, you
may still establish your attack. Remember, also,
never to play a ball without an object ! Try every
time to give such a return that it will, at the least,
make your adversary run—before she can get it ;
or if, after a long run, you find the return too difficult to place, toss it in the air as high as you can,
to give yourself time to recover your position and
your breath. Do not try and volley much—the volley game is not made for ladies ! It is too quick,
and is too great a strain on the system. But when
you are in a difficulty, and either cannot get out
of the way of the ball, or cannot run back quickly
enough to take it on the bound, then by all means
volley it : never "half volley," if you can possibly
help it ; it is a most dangerous stroke, and is
never difficult to return.

The double game, as played by two ladies on either side.

I should recommend here that both ladies play back, for the reason just quoted—viz., that a woman's weakest point in this game is volleying. Each keep to your own side, *i.e.*, right and left, putting the stronger player in the right court. This may appear at first strange advice, for you will say that this will give the adversaries an opportunity of playing on the weaker player's back-hand. If, however, your partner keeps well to the left of her court, nearly everything will come to her front-hand, and you will have the additional advantage of getting more of the game yourself. Again, to save or make the first ace is a most important point, and as you are more likely to be able to do that than your weaker partner, take the right court to enable you to do so. You may also get an extra service by these means, which is a great point, if your partner's service is weak. Play, either of you, from about between the service and base lines, and send the balls as far back into the adversaries court as possible.

Double game—gentleman and lady on either side.

Here the same argument holds good, for the gentleman to take the right court, provided he is anything of a player. If his partner is sure and steady at her returns, he may play "in" and volley; if not, he should drop back, and help her as much as possible. Let the lady remember to play at the opposite lady, and not to the gentleman adversary, as, her returns being perhaps not very difficult, he may demolish them. If her partner says "all right," or "mine," she should let the ball go to him, as he will probably make a better stroke than she will. Above all, let her pay attention, and not let her mind or eyes wander over to the other courts, or to inspect some new arrival. There is nothing more galling than to find one's partner inattentive. Another thing as lawn tennis is, never give in ! A game is never lost till it is won, and I have seen the most extraordinary games pulled off by patience, combined with plucky determination.

LAWS OF LAWN TENNIS

AS ADOPTED BY

THE M. C. C. AND THE A. E. L. T. C.

THE SINGLE-HANDED GAME.

1. For the single-handed game, the court is 27 ft. in width and 78 ft. in length. It is divided across the middle by a net, the ends of which are attached to the tops of two posts at *A* and *A*, which stand 3 ft. outside the court on each side. The height of the net is 3 ft. 6 in. at the posts, and 3 ft. at the centre. At each end of the court, parallel with the net, and at a distance of 39 ft. from it, are drawn the *base-lines CD* and *EF*, the ex-tremities of which are connected by the *side-lines CE* and *DF*. Half-way between the side-lines, and parallel with them, is drawn the *half-court-line GH*, dividing the space on each side of the net into two equal parts, called the *right* and *left courts*. On each side of the net, at a distance of 21 ft. from, and parallel with it, are drawn the *service-lines XX* and *YY*.

2. The balls shall be not less than $2\frac{1}{2}$ in. nor more than $2\frac{9}{16}$ in. in diameter ; and not less than $1\frac{7}{8}$ oz. nor more than 2 oz. in weight.

3. In matches, where umpires are appointed their decision shall be final.

4. The choice of sides and the right of serving during the first game shall be decided by toss ; provided that, if the winner of the toss choose the right to serve, the other player shall have the choice of sides, and *vice versâ*.

5. The players shall stand on opposite sides of the net : the player who first delivers the ball shall be called the *server*, the other the *striker-out*.

6. At the end of the first game, the striker-out shall become server, and the server shall become striker-out ; and so on alternately in the subsequent games of the set.

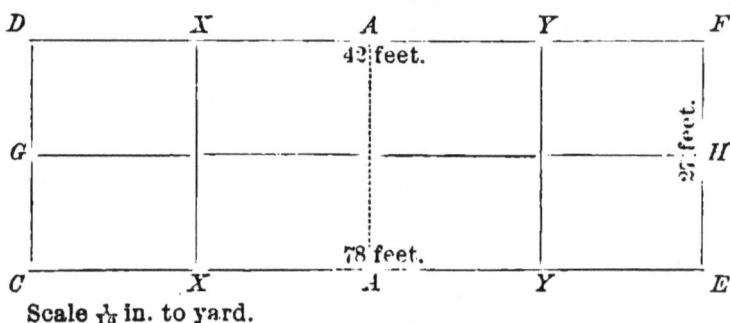

Scale 1/36 in. to yard.

SINGLE COURT.

7. The server shall serve with one foot on the baseline, with the other foot behind that line but not necessarily upon the ground, and shall deliver the service from the right and left courts alternately, beginning from the right.

8. The ball served must drop within the service-line, half-court-line, and side-line of the court, which is diagonally opposite to that from which it was served, or upon any such line.

9. It is a *fault* if the service be delivered from the wrong court, or if the server do not stand as directed in Law 7, or if the ball served drop in the net or beyond the service-line, or if it drop out of court or in the wrong court.

10. A fault may not be taken.

11. After a fault the server shall serve again from the same court from which he served that fault, unless it was a fault because served from the wrong court.

12. A fault may not be claimed after the next service has been delivered.

13. The service may not be *rolleyed*—*i.e.*, taken before it touches the ground.

14. The server shall not serve until the striker-out is ready. If the latter attempt to return the service, he shall be deemed to be ready.

15. A service or fault delivered when the striker-out is not ready counts for nothing.

16. A ball is in play from the moment at which it is delivered in service (unless a fault) until it has been rolleyed by the striker-out in his first stroke, or has dropped in the net or out of court, or has touched either of the players, or anything that he wears or carries, except his racket in the act of striking, or has been struck by either of the players with his racket more than once consecutively, or has been rolleyed before it has passed the net, or has failed to pass over the net before its first bound, or has touched the ground twice consecutively on either side of the net, though the second time may have been out of court.

17. It is a good return, although the ball touch the net ; but if the ball served touch the net, the

service, provided it be otherwise good, counts for nothing.

18. The server wins a stroke, if the striker-out volley the service, or fail to return the service, or the ball in play, or return the service or ball in play so that it drop outside any of the lines which bound his opponent's court, or otherwise lose a stroke, as provided by Law 20.

19. The striker-out wins a stroke if the server serve two consecutive faults, or fail to return the ball in play, or return the ball in play so that it drop outside any of the lines which bound his opponent's court, or otherwise lose a stroke as provided by Law 20.

20. Either player loses a stroke if the ball in play touch him or anything that he wears or carries, except his racket in the act of striking; or if he touch or strike the ball in play with his racket more than once ; or if he touch the net or any of its supports while the ball is in play ; or if he volley the ball before it has passed the net.

21. On either player winning his first stroke, the score is called 15 for that player ; on either player winning his second stroke, the score is called 30 for that player ; on either player winning his third stroke, the score is called 40 for that player ; and the fourth stroke won by either player is scored game for that player, except as below :

> If both players have won three strokes the score is called deuce ; and the next stroke won by either player is scored advantage for that player. If the same player win the next stroke, he

wins the game ; if he lose the next stroke, the game is again called deuce ; and so on until either player win the two strokes immediately following the score of deuce, when the game is scored for that player.

22. The player who first wins six games wins a set, except as below :

If both players win five games the score is called games-all ; and the next game won by either player is scored advantage game for that player. If the same player win the next game, he wins the set ; if he lose the next game, the score is again called games-all ; and so on until either player win the two games immediately following the score of games-all, when he wins the set.

Note.—Players may agree not to play advantage-sets, but to decide the set by one game after arriving at the score of games-all.

23. The players shall change sides at the end of every set ; but the umpire, on appeal from either party before the toss for choice, may direct the players to change sides at the end of every game, if, in his opinion, either side have a distinct advantage, owing to the sun, wind, or any other accidental cause ; but, if the appeal be made after a match has been begun, the umpire may only direct the players to change sides at the end of every game of the odd and concluding set.

24. When a series of sets is played, the player who was server in the last game of one set shall be striker-out in the first game of the next.

ODDS.

25. A *bisque* is one stroke, which may be claimed by the receiver of the odds at any time during a set, except as below :

A bisque may not be taken after the service has been delivered.

The server may not take a bisque after a fault, but the striker-out may do so.

26. One or more bisques may be given in augmentation or diminution of other odds.

27. *Half-fifteen* is one stroke given at the beginning of the second and every subsequent alternate game of a set.

28. *Fifteen* is one stroke given at the beginning of every game of a set.

29. *Half-thirty* is one stroke given at the beginning of the first game ; two strokes at the beginning of the second game ; and so on, alternately, in all the subsequent games of a set.

30. *Thirty* is two strokes given at the beginning of every game of a set.

31. *Half-forty* is two strokes given at the beginning of the first game ; three strokes at the beginning of the second game ; and so on, alternately, in all the subsequent games of a set.

32. *Forty* is three strokes given at the beginning of every game of a set.

33. *Half-court :* the players having agreed into which court the giver of the odds shall play, the latter loses a stroke if the ball, returned by him, drop outside any of the lines which bound that court.

THE THREE-HANDED AND FOUR-HANDED GAMES.

34. The above laws shall apply to the three-handed and four-handed games, except as below.

35. For the three-handed and four-handed games the court is 36 ft. in width. Within the side-lines, at a distance of 4½ ft. from them, and parallel with them, are drawn the service-side-lines, XY and XY. The service-lines are not drawn beyond the points XX and YY, towards the side-lines. In other respects the court is similar to that which is described in Law 1.

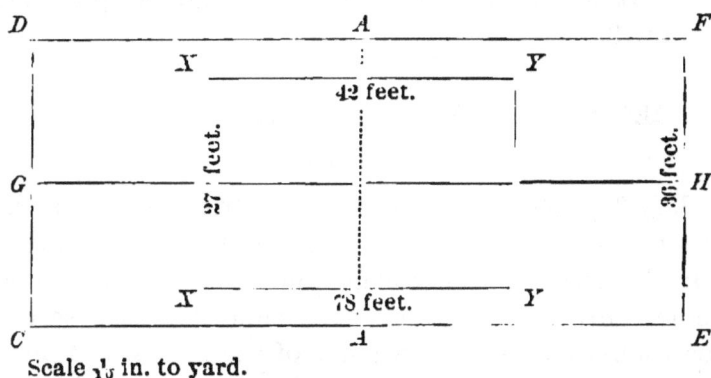

Scale $\frac{1}{15}$ in. to yard.

DOUBLE COURT.

36. In the three-handed game the simple player shall serve in every alternate game.

37. In the four-handed game the pair who have the right to serve in the first game may decide which partner shall do so, and the opposing pair may decide similarly for the second game. The partner of the player who served in the first game shall serve in the third; and the partner of the player who served in the

second game shall serve in the fourth ; and so on in the same order in all the subsequent games of a set.

38. The players shall take the service alternately throughout each game ; no player shall receive or return a service delivered to his partner ; and the order of service and of striking out, once arranged, shall not be altered, nor shall the strikers-out change courts to receive the service before the end of the set.

39. The ball served must drop within the service-line, half-court-line, and service-side-line of the court which is diagonally opposite to that from which it was served, or upon any such line.

40. It is a *fault* if the ball do not drop as provided in Law 39.

DECISIONS BY THE "FIELD," 1881–83.

SERVING.

July 30, 1881.*—There is no restriction as to the order of serving and of striking out at the beginning of a fresh set. Law 24, when applied to a four-handed game, only prescribes that the side that last served shall strike out in the first game of the next set. Which of the two players shall serve is left to their option.

It is not necessary that the server in the first game should receive the first service in the second game.

June 18, 1881.—In serving, if the ball touches one of the adversaries before it drops, it is immaterial where it would have dropped, and counts as a good service.

September 24, 1881.—In our opinion, if in the service

---

* The dates here given are those of the "Field" in which the decisions appeared.

the ball touches the server's partner, it is a fault. The ball must be deemed to have dropped as soon as it touches the partner, and consequently it has not dropped in the service-court.

November 19, 1881.—It is a fault if you strike at the ball and miss it, but not if you throw up the ball and let it drop without attempting to strike it.

February 17, 1883.—After a stroke has been decided, it is too late to object that the wrong player delivered the service.

HANDICAPS.

August 20, 1881.—There is no priority in taking a bisque.

October 22, 1881.—*A* receives fifteen in the first game of each set. What odds he had in the last game of the preceding set makes no difference.

December 3, 1881.—A player receiving fifteen must commence serving from the right-hand court.

A player who takes a bisque serves from the same court he would have served from if he had not taken it.

July 7, 1883.—Six bisques are considered equivalent to fifteen, three to half-fifteen.

July 7, 1883.—*One half-fifteen* is one stroke owed at the beginning of the *first* and every subsequent alternate game of a set.

It will thus be observed that when half odds are *received*, they are given in the second, fourth, &c., games ; and that when half odds are *owed*, they are paid in the first, third, &c., games of a set.

MISCELLANEOUS.

July 16, 1881.—It is not a let if a ball drops on another in court.

July 23, 1881.—If you or your partner touch the net while the ball is *in play*, you lose the stroke.

October 8, 1881.—It depends on whether the ball was *in play* at the moment *A* touched the net, not whether *B's* return was manifestly below the net-cord. The question of time is one of fact for the umpire to decide, and if he is unable to do so, the stroke must be played again.

June 24, 1882.—If when you volley the ball your racket is *not* over the net, you do not lose the stroke unless your racket follows over the net before the ball has left it. This is a point involving fractions of an inch, and it must be decided by sight.

July 1, 1882.—The server's partner cannot claim "not ready," but only the player served to.

July 1, 1882.—The striker loses a stroke if he volleys the ball before it has passed the net, whether he touches the net or not. In the case of a ball which has dropped and twists back over the net, it is a good return if the ball is played after it has twisted back past the net, provided the net is not touched whilst the ball is in play.

October 21, 1832.—The matches at Wimbledon are played under the laws of the M.C.C. and A.E.L.T.C. Such a score as "vantage-all" would not be allowed there.

July 7, 1883.—The player who is touched by the ball in play loses the stroke. It is immaterial whether he is standing close to the net or in the next parish.

May 12, 1883.—Either hand or both hands may be used.

June 30, 1883.—It is immaterial where the player is standing. The whole question is, Does the ball touch him before it drops ? If it does, he loses the stroke.

TABLE SHOWING METHOD OF CALCULATING DIFFERENTIAL ODDS.

For instance, *A* can give *B* 15, and can give *C* 30 ; it does not therefore follow that *B* should give *C* only 15. To make a perfect handicap, he should give him a little more, for the following reason : The game, if begun *B* 0, *C* 15, will be a longer one than if it were called *B* 15, *C* 30, which are the real points ; hence, in the longer game *B* should give *C* a trifle more than 15—the following table will show how much more, and will calculate the differential odds in all cases :

0 / C	I. (1 bisque.)	II. (2 b.)	III. (½15.)	IV. (½15+1 b.)	V. (½15+2 b.)	VI. (15.)	VII. (15+1 b.)	VIII. (15+2 b.)	IX. (½30.)	X. (½30+1 b.)	XI. (½30+2 b.)	XII. (30.)	XIII. (30+1 b.)	XIV. (30+2 b.)
C I.	0	0	0	0	0	0	0	0	0	0	0	0	0	0
D II.		0	0	0	0	0	0	1	1	1	1	1	1	
E III.			0	0	0	0	1	1	1	1	1	1	1	
F IV.				0	0	0	1	1	1	1	1	1	2	
G V.					0	0	1	1	1	1	1	2	2	
H VI.						0	1	1	1	1	2	2	2	
I VII.							0	1	1	1	2	2	2	
K VIII.								0	1	1	1	2	2	
L IX.									0	1	1	2	2	
X.										1	1	2	2	
XI.											1	1	2	
XII												1	1	
XIII.													1	

The method of working the table is as follows :

1. First of all, as six games win the best out of eleven, so six bisques are calculated to be equal to 15.

2. The figures 1, 2, 3 in the table show the number of bisques to be added to the difference between the respective odds. For example, suppose a player in class III. is drawn against a player in class IX., the difference between their respective odds is 6 bisques—*i.e.*, 15. Now, by running the eye along the third (III.) horizontal band of the table (to which III. is prefixed) until we come to the perpendicular column above which is IX., we find IX. has one (1) differential bisque from III. Hence III. gives IX. 15 + 1 bisque.

3. To take the case of A, B, and C, already quoted, and to find how much more than 15 B ought to give C, where A is scratch, giving B 15 and C 30. B, receiving 15 (or 6 bisques), is in class VI. ; similarly, C, who receives 12 bisques from scratch, is in class XII. The difference between their respective odds is 6 bisques= 15. Now find VI. in the side figures, and run your eye along till you come to the perpendicular column headed by XII. You find the figure 2=2 bisques : hence, in the case above quoted, B ought to give C 15 + 2 bisques.

4. Where the odds given exceed 30, or where the difference between the best and next best player is ½15 or more, then make the highest class above scratch— that is, make the best player begin with a minus quantity, which he has to wipe off before he can score.

5. The strength of any pair is discovered by dividing their united odds from scratch, as expressed in bisques, by 2. Thus class II. and class VIII., as partners, get 10 bisques. Divide by 2=class V. ; or, in other

words, they would get 5 bisques—*i.e.* $\frac{1}{4}15 + 2$, bisques from two scratch players.

6. If the addition of such points results in an odd number, add a bisque before dividing by 2. Thus class III. and class IV. are drawn against class VIII. and class IX. as partners—$3 + 4 = 7$. This being an odd number, add 1, which makes it 8. Similarly add 1 to $17 = 18$. Divide each by 2 now, and you get class IV. playing class IX., and giving them 5 bisques + 1 bisque differential odds, or a total of 6 bisques $= 15$.

THE END.

THE AMERICA'S CUP:

HOW IT WAS WON BY THE YACHT AMERICA IN 1851
AND HOW IT HAS BEEN SINCE DEFENDED.

By Capt. ROLAND F. COFFIN,

Author of " Sailors' Yarns," " Archibald the Cat," " How Old Wiggins Wore Ship,"
Etc , Etc.

1 vol., 12mo.   With Illustrations.   Paper, 50c.   Cloth, $1.00.

A history of all the races since 1851 for the possess'on of the trophy, the emblem of the yachting supremacy of the world—commonly called the Queen's Cup—with an account of the English yachts Genesta and Galatea, entered for the races to be sailed in September, 1885, for the possession of this most coveted prize.   Also descr p ions of the yachts Priscilla and Puritan.   There are twelve full page illustrations from drawings by Frederick S. Cozzens, an engraving of the cup, and a reproduction of John Leech's cartoon published in London *Punch* after the remarkable victory of the America in 1851.

For sale by all booksellers, or sent, post-paid, by the publishers,

CHARLES SCRIBNER'S SONS,

743 & 745 Broadway, New-York.

A

CANTERBURY PILGRIMAGE.

RIDDEN, WRITTEN AND ILLUSTRATED BY

JOSEPH AND ELIZABETH ROBINS PENNELL.

1 vol., square 8vo. Paper.

Mr. and Mrs. Pennell furnish an exceedingly entertaining story of an unconventional journey from London to Canterbury. A year ago they started off one hot August morning to make the pilgrimage, not by rail, as the latter day pilgrims usually travel, but on a tricycle. It was a merry spin through a glorious country, following the road of the famous company of bygone days. The history of the ride is most charmingly told, and the illustrations which crowd every page are in Mr. Pennell's. happiest vein.

For sale by all booksellers, or sent, post paid, by the publishers,

CHARLES SCRIBNER'S SONS,

743 & 745 Broadway, New-York.

www.ingramcontent.com/pod-product-compliance
Lightning Source LLC
Chambersburg PA
CBHW031440270326
41930CB00007B/806